Design: Jill Coote
Photography: Peter Barry
Jacket and Illustration Artwork: Jane Winton
courtesy Bernard Thornton Artists, London
Compiled by Jillian Stewart, Kate Cranshaw and Laura Potts
Edited by Josephine Bacon

**CHARTWELL BOOKS, INC.**
A Division of
**BOOK SALES, INC.**
110 Enterprise Avenue
Secaucus, New Jersey 07094

CLB 3516
© 1994 CLB Publishing
Godalming, Surrey, England
Printed and bound in Singapore
ISBN 0-7858-0144-8

# THE LITTLE BOOK ·OF·

# Herbs & Spices

*A clear, step-by-step introduction to the art of cooking with herbs and spices.*

CHARTWELL
BOOKS, INC.

# Introduction

$\mathcal{A}$ few well-chosen herbs or the addition of some spices can transform the simplest ingredients into something special, bringing a depth of flavor to otherwise ordinary dishes. A comprehensive knowledge of the flavors that different herbs and spices impart and how they should be used to bring out the very best in food is one of the greatest culinary skills, and the making of a good cook. Sadly, however, it is one of the fastest disappearing of the culinary arts. Though our forebears cultivated a wide range of both culinary and medicinal herbs and had an extensive knowledge of their properties and uses, the modern cook tends to rely on the dried, store-bought product, generally growing only a few of the most popular herbs and, in most cases, having only the sketchiest idea of their properties.

Historically, herbs and spices were used to preserve meat and fresh produce through the long winter months and helped to disguise the unpalatable taste of food that was past its best. Modern methods of preservation, particularly refrigeration, have largely seen an end to this use of herbs and spices in this way in the West (in part explaining the decline in knowledge about them) and they are used primarily to give flavor to food.

When fresh herbs are in season and are widely available they should be used in preference to dried, as they are generally – with the important exception of the bayleaf – superior in taste. Basil, in particular, should be eaten fresh as it is one of the few herbs that cannot

be dried successfully. As the flavor of fresh herbs can be easily impaired it is important to prepare and use them properly. The oils which are contained in the plant and are released when it is broken up or heated, imparting the unique flavor of the herb to the food, can be easily spoiled. To minimize the risk of this happening, use your fingers to tear the herbs where directed, rather than chopping them with a knife. Follow instructions about when to add them to the recipe carefully, ensuring that they are not added too soon or too late. If you are using dried herbs, it is important to remember that they are more concentrated in their flavor than fresh, and should be used in smaller quantities.

Spices, which are the dried seeds, pods, berries, roots, stems, or buds of aromatic plants, have played an important part in the culinary traditions of many nations. Like dried herbs, pre-ground spices are widely available in the stores. For the best results, however, it is best to grind your own. If you are buying pre-ground spices, do not buy them in large quantities and store them in a dark place rather than in direct sunlight as they lose their flavor quickly.

This book offers a delicious selection of recipes that use a wide range of herbs and spices in many different styles of cookery, and is thus the perfect introduction to the delights of cooking with herbs and spices. It features some of the lesser-known and more unusual herbs and spices, as well as the more popular and frequently used varieties.

# Dolmades

### SERVES 6-8

*These Greek delicacies can be served with plain yogurt or a tomato sauce.*

PREPARATION: 30 mins
COOKING: 40 mins

---

2 cups fresh grape leaves or leaves packed in
    brine
¾ cup cooked long-grain rice
8 scallions (green onions), finely chopped
1½ tbsps chopped fresh dill
3 tbsps chopped fresh mint
1 tbsp chopped fresh parsley
4 tbsps pine nuts (piñons)
4 tbsps currants
Salt and pepper
⅔ cup virgin olive oil
Juice of 1 lemon

---

**1.** If using fresh grape leaves, put them into boiling water for about 1 minute. Remove and drain. If using preserved grape leaves, rinse them and then place in a bowl of hot water 5 minutes to soak. Strain and pat dry.

**Step 3** Spread the leaves out on a flat surface. Place spoonfuls of stuffing on the leaves and make into a sausage shape.

**Step 4** Fold the sides over the filling and roll up the leaves.

**2.** Mix together all the remaining ingredients, except the olive oil and lemon juice. Taste the filling and adjust the seasoning if necessary.

**3.** Spread the grape leaves out on a flat surface, vein side upward. Cut off the stems and place about 2 tsps of filling on each leaf, pressing it into a sausage shape.

**4.** Fold the sides of the leaves over to partially cover the stuffing and roll up as for a jellyroll. Place the rolls, seam side down, in a large saucepan. Pour the olive oil and lemon juice over them.

**5.** Pour hot water over the rolls until it comes about halfway up their sides. Place a plate on top of the rolls to keep them in place, cover the pan and cook slowly about 40 minutes.

**6.** Remove the Dolmades to a serving platter and accompany with lemon wedges, black olives, and plain yogurt if wished.

# Mussels in Red Wine

*SERVES 4*

*Red wine makes an unusual, but very pleasant combination with seafood. This recipe is equally good with clams.*

PREPARATION: 30 mins, plus 2 hrs chilling
COOKING: 10 mins

---

1¼ cups dry red wine
3 pounds mussels, well scrubbed
6 tbsps olive oil
4 cloves garlic, finely chopped
2 bayleaves
2 tbsps fresh thyme, chopped
6 tbsps red wine vinegar
1 tsp paprika
Grated rind and juice of 1 lemon
Salt and pepper
Pinch cayenne pepper
Chopped parsley

---

**1.** Place the wine in a large saucepan and bring to the boil. Add the mussels, cover the pan, and cook briskly about 4-5 minutes,

**Step 1** Cook the mussels over high heat, stirring frequently, until the shells begin to open.

**Step 4** Remove the mussels from their shells with your fingers or using a teaspoon.

stirring frequently, until the shells open. Discard any that do not open.

**2.** Transfer the mussels to a bowl. Strain the cooking liquid through a fine sieve lined with cheesecloth and reserve it.

**3.** In a clean saucepan, heat the oil and sauté the garlic over a gentle heat until golden-brown. Add the bayleaves, thyme, vinegar, paprika, lemon juice and rind, salt and pepper, and cayenne pepper. Add the wine, and bring to the boil. Cook to reduce to about ⅔ cup. Allow to cool completely.

**4.** Remove the mussels from their shells and add them to the liquid, stirring to coat all the mussels. Cover and refrigerate at least 2 hours. Allow to stand at room temperature about 30 minutes before serving. Sprinkle with chopped parsley.

# Spaghetti with Basil Sauce (Pesto)

*SERVES 4*

*Home-made Pesto tastes much better than any brand you can
buy in the supermarket.*

PREPARATION: 5 mins
COOKING: 15 mins

---

8 tbsps extra-virgin olive oil
2 cloves garlic, peeled
3 tbsps pine nuts (piñons)
1 cup fresh basil leaves
3 tbsps grated Parmesan cheese
Salt and pepper
10 ounces spaghetti
Extra basil leaves for garnish

---

**1.** Heat 1 tablespoon of the oil in a small skillet over a low heat. Add the garlic and pine nuts, and cook until the nuts are pale golden. Drain.

**2.** Finely chop the basil leaves, pine nuts, and garlic in a food processor or blender.

**3.** When smooth, add the remaining oil in a thin stream, blending continuously.

**4.** Transfer the mixture to a bowl; mix in the grated cheese, and add salt and pepper to taste.

**5.** Meanwhile, cook the spaghetti in a large pan of boiling salted water 10 minutes, or until just tender.

**6.** Drain, and serve with the basil sauce tossed through, and a side dish of grated cheese. Garnish with fresh basil.

# Spinach and Cheese Pie

*SERVES 6-12*

*This classic Greek pie is simplicity itself thanks to ready-made phyllo dough, available from Greek delicatessens.*

PREPARATION: 25 mins
COOKING: 40 mins

---

1 pound package phyllo dough
2 pounds fresh spinach
3 tbsps olive oil
2 onions, finely chopped
3 tbsps chopped fresh dill
3 eggs, slightly beaten
Salt and pepper
1 cup feta cheese, crumbled
½ cup butter

---

**1.** Unfold the dough on a flat surface and cut it to fit the size of the baking dish to be used. Keep the dough covered.

**2.** Tear the stalks off the spinach and wash the leaves well. Shred the leaves with a sharp knife.

**3.** Heat the oil in a large skillet and cook the onions until soft. Add the spinach and stir over a medium heat about 5 minutes. Increase the heat to evaporate any moisture.

**4.** Allow the spinach and onions to cool. Mix in the dill, eggs, salt and pepper, and cheese.

**5.** Melt the butter and brush the baking dish on the bottom and sides. Butter the top sheet of

**Step 5** To assemble the pie, butter the base and sides of the dish and then butter each layer of dough before stacking them up in the dish.

phyllo dough and place it in the dish. Butter another sheet and place that on top of the first. Repeat to make 8 layers of dough.

**6.** Spread on the filling and cover the top with 6 or 7 layers of dough, brushing each layer with melted butter. Butter the top layer well and score the dough in square or diamond shapes. Do not cut through to the bottom layer.

**7.** Sprinkle with a little water and bake in an oven preheated to 375°F for 40 minutes or until crisp and golden.

**8.** Leave the pie to stand about 10 minutes and then cut through the scoring completely to the bottom layer. Lift out the pieces to a serving platter.

# Szechuan Fish

SERVES 6

*The piquant spiciness of Szechuan pepper is quite different from that of black or white pepper.*

PREPARATION: 20 mins
COOKING: 10 mins

1 pound white fish fillets, skinned
1 egg
5 tbsps all-purpose flour
6 tbsps white wine
Oil for frying
½ cup cooked ham, diced
1-inch fresh ginger root, finely diced
½-1 red or green chili, seeded and finely diced
6 water chestnuts, finely diced
4 green onions (scallions), finely chopped
3 tbsps light soy sauce
1 tsp cider vinegar or rice wine vinegar
½ tsp ground Szechuan pepper
1¼ cups chicken broth
1 tbsp cornstarch dissolved with 2 tbsps water
2 tsps sugar

**1.** Cut the fish into 2-inch pieces. Beat the egg and add the flour and wine to make a batter.

**2.** Heat enough oil in a wok to deep-fry the fish. Dredge the fish lightly with seasoned flour and then dip into the batter. Fry a few pieces of fish at a time, until golden-brown.

To garnish, slit chilies from the tip towards the stems. Stand in iced water until curled.

**3.** Remove all but 1 tbsp of oil from the wok and add the ham, ginger, diced chili, water chestnuts, and green onions (scallions). Cook about 1 minute then add the soy sauce, vinegar, and Szechuan pepper. Stir well and cook a further minute. Remove the vegetables from the wok and set them aside.

**4.** Add the broth to the wok and bring to the boil. Add 1 tbsp of the broth to the cornstarch mixture. Add the mixture back to the broth and reboil, stirring constantly until thickened.

**5.** Stir in the sugar and add the fish and vegetables to the sauce. Heat through for 30 seconds and serve at once.

# Pasta and Asparagus Salad

*SERVES 4*

*This elegant green salad is a wonderful way of making the most of asparagus, that most luxurious of vegetables.*

PREPARATION: 15 mins
COOKING: 20 mins

4 ounces fettucini
1 pound asparagus, trimmed and cut into 1-inch pieces
2 zucchini, cut into 2-inch sticks
2 tbsps chopped fresh parsley
2 tbsps chopped fresh marjoram
1 lemon, peeled and segmented
Grated rind and juice of 1 lemon
6 tbsps extra-virgin olive oil
Pinch of sugar
Salt and freshly ground black pepper
Lettuce leaves

**1.** Cook the pasta in plenty of lightly-salted boiling water 10 minutes or as directed on the package.

**2.** Drain and rinse briefly in cold water. Drain again and leave to cool completely.

**3.** Cook the asparagus in lightly-salted boiling water 4 minutes, then add the zucchini, and cook a further 3-4 minutes or until the vegetables are just tender. Drain, and rinse briefly in cold water. Drain again and leave to cool.

**4.** Place the cooked pasta, vegetables, herbs, and lemon segments in a large bowl and mix together, taking care to keep the vegetables whole.

**5.** Mix together the lemon rind and juice, oil, sugar, and salt and pepper to make the dressing.

**6.** Arrange the lettuce on serving plates. Just before serving pour the dressing over the vegetables and pasta, and toss to coat well.

**7.** Pile equal quantities of the pasta salad into the center of the salad leaves and serve immediately.

# Trout with Chive Sauce

*SERVES 4*

*Chives added to a cream and wine sauce make a delicious accompaniment to trout.*

PREPARATION: 15 mins
COOKING: 15-20 mins

---

4 rainbow trout, cleaned
4 tbsps melted butter
2 tbsps white wine
3¾ cups heavy cream
1 small bunch chives, snipped
Salt and pepper

---

**1.** Dredge the trout with the seasoned flour and place on a lightly-greased baking tray.

**2.** Spoon the melted butter over the fish, and bake in an oven preheated to 400°F about 10 minutes.

**3.** Baste frequently with the butter, and cook until the skin is crisp. Check the fish on the underside close to the bone to see if it is done.

**4.** If the fish is not cooked through, lower the oven temperature to 325°F and cook a further 5 minutes.

**5.** Pour the wine into a small saucepan and bring to the boil. Boil to reduce by half.

**6.** Add the cream and bring back to the boil. Allow to boil rapidly until the cream thickens slightly.

**7.** Stir in the snipped chives, reserving some to sprinkle on top, if wished.

**8.** When the fish are browned, remove to a serving dish and spoon over some of the sauce.

**9.** Sprinkle with the reserved chives and serve the rest of the sauce separately.

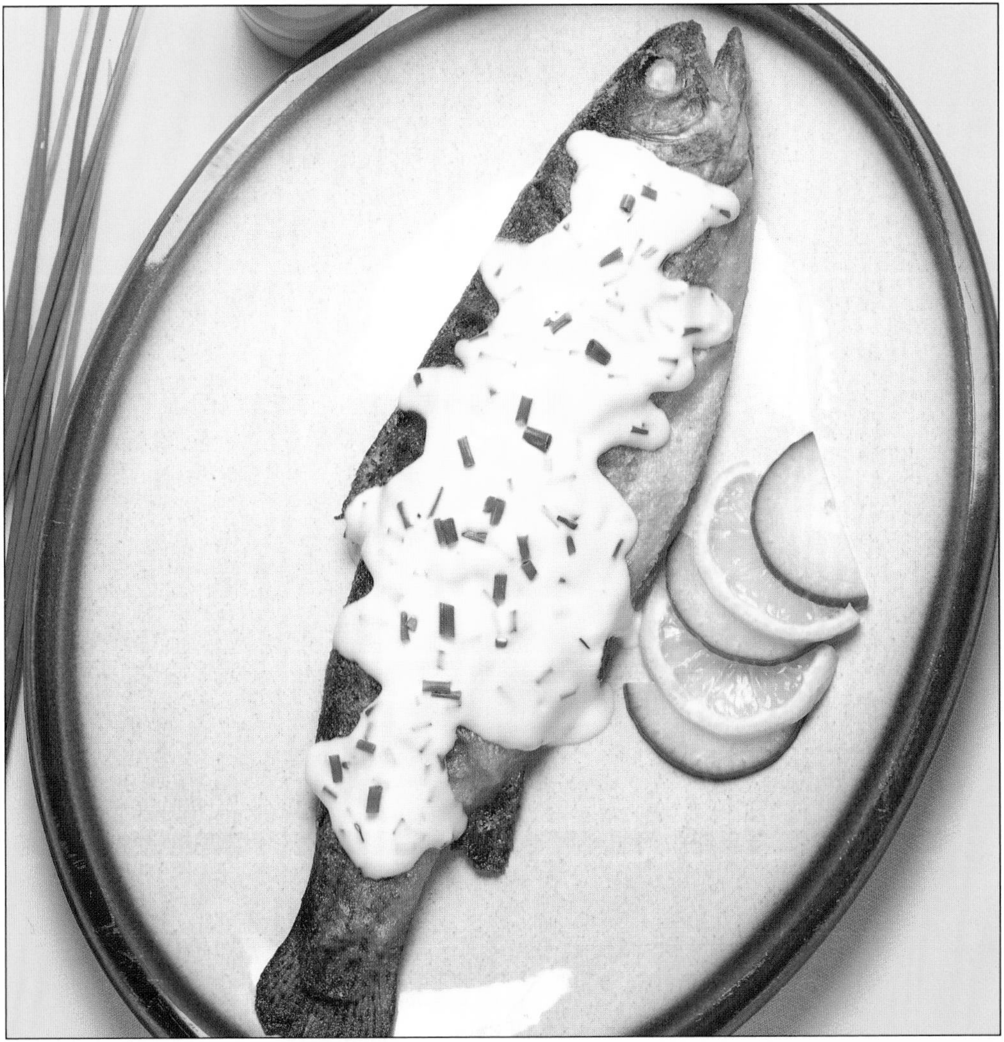

# Rogan Josh

*This recipe originates from Kashmir, the northernmost state in India.*

PREPARATION: 20 mins
COOKING: 1½ hrs

3 tbsps ghee or clarified butter
2¼ pounds boneless leg of lamb, cut into 1½
  -inch cubes
1 tbsp ground cumin
1 tbsp ground coriander
1 tsp ground turmeric
1 tsp chili powder
1-inch cube of root ginger, peeled and grated
2-4 cloves garlic, crushed
1 cup finely sliced onions
14-ounce can tomatoes, chopped
1 tbsp tomato paste
½ cup warm water
1¼ tsps salt or to taste
⅓ cup whipping cream
2 tsps garam masala or curry powder
2 tbsps chopped coriander (cilantro) leaves

**1.** Melt 2 tbsps of the ghee over a medium heat and fry the meat in batches until it changes color. Remove with a slotted spoon and keep aside.

**2.** Lower the heat to minimum and add the spices, ginger, and garlic; stir and sauté 30 seconds.

**3.** Add the meat, plus any juice, stir and fry over a medium heat 3-4 minutes. Add the onions and fry 5-6 minutes, stirring frequently.

**4.** Add the tomatoes and tomato paste – stir and cook 2-3 minutes.

**5.** Add the water and salt, bring to the boil, cover and simmer about 1 hour, or until the meat is tender.

**6.** Stir in the cream and remove from the heat.

**7.** In a separate pan, melt the remaining ghee over a medium heat. Add the garam masala or curry powder, stir briskly, and add to the meat.

**8.** Rinse the pan out with a little meat gravy to ensure that any remaining garam masala or curry powder and ghee mixture is added to the meat. Mix well and stir in the coriander leaves.

# Roast Pork Wild Game-Style

## SERVES 6-8

*The love of game is part of Polish culinary history and even meat from reared animals was cooked like game. The marinating takes two days.*

PREPARATION: 20 mins, plus 2 days marinating
COOKING: 2¼ hrs

3 pounds boneless pork roast
2 tbsps lard or cooking fat
Paprika
1 tsp flour
⅔ cup sour cream or plain thick-set yogurt
1 tbsp chopped fresh dill

*Marinade*
1 carrot, finely chopped
2 celery sticks, finely chopped
1 bayleaf
5 black peppercorns
5 allspice berries
2 sprigs thyme
10 juniper berries, slightly crushed
2 onions, sliced
4 tbsps dry white wine
Juice and grated rind of 1 lemon

*Beet Sauce*
2 pounds cooked beets, peeled
4 tbsps butter or margarine
2 tbsps all-purpose flour
1 onion, minced
1 clove garlic, crushed
⅔ cup chicken broth
Sugar, salt and pepper
White wine vinegar

**1.** Combine the marinade ingredients in a saucepan and bring to the boil. Allow to cool. Place the pork in a bowl and pour the marinade over it. Cover and refrigerate two days, turning the meat frequently. Remove the meat and wipe it dry with kitchen paper. Reserve the marinade.

**2.** Heat the lard in a roasting pan. Sprinkle the fat side of the pork with paprika, and brown it on all sides. Cook, uncovered, in an oven preheated to 375°F for two hours. Pour the marinade over the meat after one hour. Baste frequently with the pan juices.

**3.** Remove the pork from the pan and keep warm. Skim any fat from the sauce and strain the vegetables and juice into a pan. Mix the flour, sour cream, and dill together and add to the pan. Bring just to the boil, then simmer 1-2 minutes.

**4.** Shred the beets or cut into small dice. Melt the butter in a saucepan and add the flour and onion. Stir well and cook over a moderate heat until light brown. Add the garlic, and stir in the broth gradually.

**5.** Bring to the boil, add the beets, sugar, salt, pepper, and vinegar to taste. Cook 10 minutes over a moderate heat, stirring occasionally.

**6.** To serve, slice the pork and pour the sauce over it. Serve with the beets.

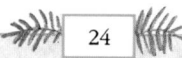

# Chicken Mughlai with Coriander Chutney

## SERVES 4-6

*The creamy spiciness of the chicken contrasts with the hotness of the chutney in this Indian dish.*

PREPARATION: 25 mins
COOKING: 30-40 mins

---

4 tbsps oil
3 pounds chicken pieces, skinned
1 tsp ground cardamom
½ tsp ground cinnamon
1 bayleaf
4 cloves
2 onions, minced
1-inch piece fresh ginger root, grated
4 cloves garlic, crushed
2 tbsps ground almonds
2 tsps cumin seeds
Pinch cayenne pepper
1¼ cups cream
6 tbsps plain yogurt
2 tbsps roasted cashew nuts
2 tbsps golden raisins

*Chutney*
3 ounce fresh coriander (cilantro)
1 green chili, chopped and seeded
1 tbsp lemon juice
Salt and pepper
Pinch sugar
1 tbsp oil
½ tsp ground coriander (cilantro)

---

**1.** Heat the oil in a large skillet, add the chicken pieces, and fry on each side until golden.

**2.** Remove the chicken and set aside. Put the cardamom, cinnamon, bayleaf, and cloves into the hot oil and meat juices. Fry 30 seconds. Stir in the onions and sauté until soft but not brown.

**3.** Add the ginger, garlic, almonds, cumin, and cayenne pepper. Cook gently for 2-3 minutes, then stir in the cream.

**4.** Return the chicken pieces to the pan, along with any juices. Cover, and simmer gently 30-40 minutes, or until the chicken is cooked and tender.

**5.** Meanwhile prepare the chutney. Put the coriander leaves, chili, lemon, seasoning, and sugar into a blender or food processor and grind to a paste.

**6.** Heat the oil and cook the ground coriander 1 minute. Add this to the coriander leaves and blend in thoroughly.

**7.** Just before serving, stir the yogurt, cashews, and yellow raisins into the chicken. Heat through just enough to make the yellow raisins swell, but do not allow the mixture to boil.

**8.** Serve at once with the coriander chutney.

# Tomato Beef Stir-Fry

*SERVES 4*

*East meets West in a dish that is lightning-fast to cook and tastes like a barbecue stir fry.*

PREPARATION: 20 mins, plus 4 hours marinating
COOKING: 20-25 mins

1 pound round-eye or rib-eye steak
2 cloves garlic, crushed
6 tbsps wine vinegar
6 tbsps oil
Pinch sugar
Salt and pepper
1 bayleaf
1 tbsp ground cumin
1 small red bell pepper, sliced
1 small green bell pepper, sliced
Oil for frying
½ cup baby sweetcorn
4 green onions (scallions), shredded

*Tomato sauce*
4 tbsps oil
1 medium onion, finely chopped
1-2 green chilies, finely chopped
1-2 cloves garlic, crushed
8 fresh ripe tomatoes, skinned, seeded, and
   chopped
3 tbsps tomato paste
6 sprigs fresh coriander (cilantro)

**1.** Slice the meat thinly across the grain.

**Step 3** Cook the meat quickly over high heat to brown.

Combine in a plastic bag with the next 6 ingredients. Tie the bag and toss the ingredients inside to coat. Place in a bowl and leave about 4 hours.

**2.** Heat the oil for the sauce and cook the onion, chilies, and garlic to soften but not brown. Add the remaining sauce ingredients and cook about 15 minutes over a gentle heat. Purée in a food processor until smooth.

**3.** Heat a skillet and add the meat in three batches, discarding the marinade. Cook to brown and set aside. Add about 2 tbsps oil and cook the peppers about 2 minutes.

**4.** Add the corn and onions and return the meat to the pan. Cook for a further minute and add the sauce. Cook to heat through and serve immediately.

# Chicken Escalopes

*SERVES 4*

*Although this is one of the simplest methods of cooking chicken, it is also one of the most delicious.*

PREPARATION: 20 mins
COOKING: 12-16 mins

4 chicken breasts, boned and skinned
1 egg white
8 tbsps wholewheat breadcrumbs
1 tbsp chopped fresh sage
Salt and freshly ground black pepper
2 tbsps walnut oil
½ cup mayonnaise
⅔ cup plain low-fat yogurt
1 tsp grated fresh horseradish
2 tbsps chopped walnuts
Lemon slices and chopped walnuts, to garnish

**1.** Pat the chicken breasts dry with kitchen paper.

**2.** Whisk the egg whites with a fork until they just begin to froth, but are still liquid.

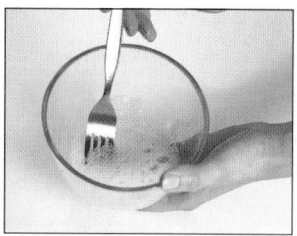

**Step 2** Whisk the egg white with a fork until it is frothy, but still liquid.

**Step 5** Press the bread-crumb mixture onto the chicken breasts, making sure that they are covered evenly.

**3.** Carefully brush all surfaces of the chicken breasts with the beaten egg white.

**4.** Put the breadcrumbs onto a shallow plate and mix in the chopped sage and seasoning.

**5.** Place the chicken breasts, one at a time, on the crumbs, and carefully press the mixture onto the chicken.

**6.** Heat the oil in a large skillet, and gently sauté the prepared chicken breasts on each side 6-8 minutes, or until they are golden and tender. Set them aside, and keep warm.

**7.** Mix all the remaining ingredients, except for the garnish, in a small bowl, whisking well to blend the yogurt and mayonnaise evenly.

**8.** Place the cooked chicken breasts on a serving dish, and spoon a little of the sauce over them. Serve garnished with the lemon slices and additional chopped nuts.

# Herb Rice Pilaff

*SERVES 6*

*Fresh herbs are a must for this rice dish, but use whatever mixture suits your taste or complements the main course.*

PREPARATION: 20 mins
COOKING: 20-25 mins

2 tbsps oil
2 tbsps butter
¾ cup uncooked long-grain rice
2½ cups boiling water
Pinch salt and pepper
1 cup mixed chopped fresh herbs (parsley, thyme, marjoram, basil)
1 small bunch green onions (scallions), finely chopped

**1.** Heat the oil in a large, heavy-based saucepan and add the butter. When foaming,

**Step 1** Cook the rice in the oil and butter until it begins to turn opaque.

**Step 3** Cook very gently about 20 minutes, or until all the liquid has been absorbed by the rice, and the grains are tender.

add the rice and cook over a moderate heat about 2 minutes, stirring constantly.

**2.** When the rice begins to look opaque, add the water, salt, and pepper, and bring to the boil, stirring occasionally.

**3.** Cover the pan and reduce the heat. Simmer very gently, without stirring, about 20 minutes or until all the liquid has been absorbed and the rice is tender.

**4.** Chop the herbs very finely and stir into the rice along with the chopped green onions. Cover the pan and leave to stand about 5 minutes before serving.

# Herbed Vegetable Strips

## SERVES 4

*Fresh basil and parsley mixed with tender-crisp vegetables and nuts make a delicious side-dish.*

PREPARATION: 30-40 mins
COOKING: 10 mins

2 large zucchini, ends trimmed
2 medium carrots, peeled
1 large or 2 small leeks, trimmed, halved, and
    well washed
1 cup walnuts
1 small onion, chopped
2 tbsps chopped parsley
2 tbsps chopped basil
1¼-2 cups olive oil
Salt and pepper

**1.** Cut the zucchini and carrots into long, thin slices with a mandolin or by hand. A food processor will work but the slices will be short.

**2.** Cut the leeks into lengths the same size as the zucchini and carrots. Make sure the leeks are well rinsed in between all layers. Cut into long, thin strips.

**3.** Using a large, sharp knife, cut the zucchini and carrot slices into long, thin strips about the thickness of 2 matchsticks. The julienne blade of a food processor will produce strips that are too fine to use.

**4.** Place the carrot strips in a pan of boiling salted water and cook about 3-4 minutes or until tender-crisp. Drain and rinse under cold

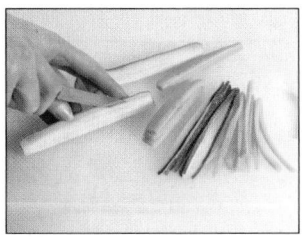

**Step 3** Stack up several lengths of zucchini and carrot and cut into long julienne strips.

water. Cook the zucchini strips separately about 2-3 minutes and add the leek strips during the last minute of cooking. Drain and rinse the vegetables and leave with the carrots to drain dry.

**5.** Place the walnuts, onion, parsley, and basil in the bowl of a food processor or in a blender and chop finely.

**6.** Reserve about 3 tbsps of the olive oil for later use. With the machine running, pour the rest of the oil through the funnel in a thin, steady stream. Use enough oil to bring the mixture to the consistency of mayonnaise. Add seasoning to taste.

**7.** Heat the reserved oil in a large pan and add the vegetables. Season and toss over moderate heat until heated through. Add the herb-and-walnut sauce and toss gently to coat the vegetables. Serve immediately.

# Spiced Crème Brûlée

*SERVES 4*

*These rich, creamy desserts make a perfect end to a dinner party.*

PREPARATION: 15 mins
COOKING: 20 mins

---

4 egg yolks
1½ tbsps cornstarch
⅓ cup sugar
1¼ cups milk
1¼ cups heavy cream
1 stick cinnamon
2 tsps coriander seed, slightly crushed
1 vanilla bean
Light brown sugar

---

**1.** Beat the egg yolks, cornstarch, and sugar together until pale.

**2.** Heat the milk, cream, spices, and vanilla bean just to boiling point then gradually strain onto the egg yolk mixture, beating constantly.

**3.** Return the custard to the rinsed-out pan and place over a gentle heat. Bring the mixture to the boil, stirring constantly.

**4.** When the mixture coats the back of the spoon, remove from the heat. Do not allow to boil rapidly.

**5.** Strain into 4 individual soufflé dishes. The custard should come almost to the top. Chill until set.

**6.** Put the custards into a roasting pan and surround with ice. Sprinkle a thin layer of the light brown sugar over the top of each custard and put under a very hot broiler.

**7.** Rotate the dishes and move the pan around until the sugar melts and caramelizes.

**8.** Chill until the sugar layer is hard and crisp.

# Guava Mint Sorbet

*MAKES 850ml/1½ pints*
*The exotic taste of guava works well with mint.*

PREPARATION: 2-3 hrs, including freezing

¾ cup sugar
1¼ cups water
4 ripe guavas
2 tbsps chopped fresh mint
Freshly squeezed lime juice
1 egg white
Fresh mint leaves, for decoration

**1.** Combine the sugar and water in a heavy-based saucepan and bring slowly to the boil to dissolve the sugar. When the mixture is a clear sirup, boil rapidly 30 seconds. Allow to cool to room temperature and then chill in the refrigerator.

**2.** Cut the guavas in half and scoop out the

**Step 3** Freeze the mixture until slushy and then process to break up the ice crystals.

**Step 4** Process the frozen mixture again and gradually work in the egg white.

pulp. Discard the skins and seeds, and purée the fruit in a food processor until smooth. Add the mint and combine with the cold sirup. Add lime juice until the right balance of sweetness is reached.

**3.** Pour the mixture into a shallow container and freeze until slushy. Process again to break up the ice crystals and then freeze until firm.

**4.** Whisk the egg white until stiff but not dry. Process the sorbet again and when smooth, fold in the egg white. Freeze again until firm.

**5.** Remove from the freezer 15 minutes before serving and keep in the refrigerator.

**6.** Arrange scoops of the sorbet in dessert glasses and decorate each serving with mint.

# Cinnamon Cœur à la Crème
# with Raspberry Sauce

*SERVES 4*

*Delicious cinnamon creams are complemented delightfully
by the sharp raspberry sauce.*

PREPARATION: 15 mins, plus 8 hrs chilling

1 cup cream cheese
1½ cups whipping cream
1 cup confectioner's sugar, sifted
2 tsps ground cinnamon
2 cups fresh raspberries

**1.** Put the cream cheese into a large bowl along with 4 tbsps of the cream. Whisk with an electric mixer until the mixture is light and fluffy.

**2.** Mix in ⅓ cup of the confectioner's sugar and the cinnamon, stirring well until all ingredients are well blended.

**3.** Whip the remaining cream until it forms soft peaks, then fold into the cheese mixture with a metal spoon.

**4.** Line four individual heart-shaped molds with dampened cheesecloth or clean damp J-cloths, extending the cloth beyond the edges of the molds.

**5.** Spoon the cheese mixture into the molds

**Step 6** Stand the molds on a rack over a tray to collect the drips when refrigerated.

and spread out evenly, pressing down well to remove any air bubbles.

**6.** Fold the overlapping edges of the cloth over the top of the mixture, and refrigerate the molds on a rack placed over a tray, for at least 8 hours.

**7.** Purée the raspberries in a liquidizer or food processor, and press through a nylon sieve to remove all the seeds. Blend in the remaining confectioner's sugar to sweeten.

**8.** Turn out the molds onto four dessert plates, and carefully remove the cloth. Spoon a little of the sauce over each heart and serve the remainder separately.

# Chocolate Spice Cake

*MAKES 1 × 8-INCH CAKE*

*What a difference! The addition of spices sets this cake apart from ordinary chocolate cakes.*

PREPARATION: 30 mins
COOKING: 40-45 mins

5 eggs, separated
6 tbsps superfine sugar
3 squares plain chocolate, melted
6 tbsps all-purpose flour ⎫
½ tsp ground nutmeg ⎪
½ tsp ground cinnamon ⎬ sifted together
½ tsp ground cloves ⎭

*Topping*
1 tbsp confectioner's sugar
1 tsp ground cinnamon

**1.** Grease and line an 8-inch springform pan with parchment paper.

**2.** Brush the paper with melted butter and dust with a little flour.

**Step 8** Mix together the confectioner's sugar and cinnamon and sieve this over the cake.

**3.** Put the egg yolks and sugar into a mixing bowl and whisk vigorously until the mixture is thick and creamy.

**4.** Stir in the melted chocolate and fold in the flour and spices using a metal spoon.

**5.** Whisk the egg whites until they form soft peaks. Fold these carefully into the chocolate mixture.

**6.** Pour the cake mixture into the prepared pan and bake in a pre-heated oven at 350°F, for 40-45 minutes, or until a skewer inserted into the middle of the cake comes out clean.

**7.** Leave the cake to cool in the pan for 10 minutes, then unmold onto a wire rack and leave to cool completely.

**8.** Mix together the confectioner's sugar and cinnamon. Sieve this over the top of the cake, before serving.

**Step 3** Whisk the egg yolks and sugar together vigorously, until they are thick and creamy.

# Index

Spaghetti with Basil and Pesto Sauce